How to Think Like a Spy

Spy Secrets and Survival Techniques That Can Save You and Your Family

Table of Contents

in any fashion deemed liable for any hardship or damages that may befall them after undertaking information described herein.

Additionally, the information in the following pages is intended only for informational purposes and should thus be thought of as universal. As befitting its nature, it is presented without assurance regarding its prolonged validity or interim quality. Trademarks that are mentioned are done without written consent and can in no way be considered an endorsement from the trademark holder.

Introduction

Congratulations on purchasing *How to Think Like a Spy*.

Whether you were looking for a fun read or seeking detailed and under the radar information regarding what it takes to become a successful spy, then you are in for a real treat!

Each of the chapters in this book will go through the most crucial areas of expertise that today's spies in action must have. While the television shows that you avidly watch may give you a good look at the everyday agendas of the average spy, they really do not do a great job at portraying a realistic standpoint. This book will help you to dive right into the back pocket of what a run-of-the-mill spy does as they fulfill missions, save the world, and make the world a better place to dwell!

You never know when you will fall into a delicate predicament that will require knowledge beyond your reach. The information within this book will help you to survive unique situations and will mold you into a more observant human being.

While there might be a few books on the life of

a spy, this is the only one written in a friendly, everyday tone that will help the average Joe become a seasoned agent in their free time. This book is all about developing the proper mindset that is required of one to make themselves into a prosperous detective.

Thanks again for purchasing this book. Every effort was made to ensure it is full of as much useful, valuable, and fun-to-read information as possible. Please enjoy reading and have fun learning what it takes to become a spy!

Thinking to Survive

The main aspect of becoming a successful spy is having the ability to successfully get your mind into the proper mindset to function in a variety of stressful situations.

Learning to Manage Stressful Situations

Let's take a moment to think about what separates those that survive and those that become victims of disasters and dangerous situations. Survivors tend to have these aspects on their side, along with a possible stroke of luck:

- Ability to hone in on the task at hand

- Not stressed by having to think outside-the-box

- Understand clearly what needs to be done

- Can respond quickly

Having a survival mindset in your back pocket will not only make actions much easier to do, but will reduce effects of crisis, such as shock, panic, and fatigue. Those that immediately have the mindset that they are going to die or get hurt are less likely to take logical action and rely on "pre-programmed" responses rather than taking action as a scenario unfolds. This means they are more likely to become emotionally and mentally stressed, leaving them incapable of surviving.

Survival is all about keeping your ego in check, managing emotions, and controlling your fears. Spies of all kinds put themselves in the face of danger on a regular basis and must be prepared to cultivate the proper mindset to survive. This means going beyond having just good equipment to battle hardships. This section will provide what you will need to develop a healthy mindset that will increase your chances of withstanding both short and long-term crisis.

Overcoming Fear

The response you have to stressful situations greatly determines how you overcome the challenges that you are presented with. The key to survival is learning how to control your fears. In many folks exposed to crisis, they find themselves frozen where they stand, unable to take action. In others, fear provokes our natural "flight-or-fight" response, which can cause one to make wrong and tragic decisions because they jump to conclusions too quickly. For those that are fortunate enough to be able to survive situations and take a look back to an unfortunate event, they are able to clearly see what fears held them back and robbed them of their common sense.

Here are some tips to get control over fear:

- Analyze what makes you afraid. When you know your fears inside and out, you can learn how to train yourself to get the confidence you need to face those fears head-on in crisis.

- If you choose to fear your fears, you are only giving in to what weakens you, making you far more vulnerable. If you take the time to evaluate your fears, you will see what makes you scared and conquer it head on.

- Ego has no place in stressful scenarios. If you are in the mindset of thinking you are constantly right, there is more than likely a nice fear that is hiding right underneath that ego. Being fearful of possibly being wrong gives you less chance of survival. Do not assume that what you know will always work or that you know everything about the situation at hand. Fear drives ego. When things do not go as planned, this same fear will eventually lead to destruction or possible death.

Have a Positive Outlook

Seems kind of silly, doesn't it? How could positivity outlive the potential for dying? Positivity breathes life into the ability to successfully function in stressful situations, which is why it's a good idea to practice having a positive outlook on a *daily* basis.

Begin each and every day on a positive note, with a confident though. Pick a phrase that uplifts you, and mentally say it to yourself. When faced with fears or stress, your chosen phrase can play a big part in getting yourself through not only the scenario unraveling but also through the storm of emotions that your body is experiencing during a dangerous situation. Positivity allows one to get into a state of mind where they can process what is occurring and respond efficiently without fear getting in the way of survival.

Assessing Danger with Accuracy

Being hyper-vigilant of imminent danger will only lead to making terrible decisions and possible paranoia. Never allow your imagination cloud your common sense that is required to survive. While you should not become forgetful that you are in danger, do not let that idea take control of your actions and the ability to make good decisions.

Understand Peer Pressure

Peer pressure is far more powerful than you think. If can make a perfectly sane individual doubt their own intelligence, causing them to make poor decisions and take actions that might put them at higher risk. Peer pressure lies heavily in society, making strong suggestions at what we should be thinking, feeling, wearing, perceiving the world, etc.

Outrun peer pressure and don't let it prevent you from thinking what you want about the things happening in the world around you. Be consciously aware of the aspects of peer pressure and how they can directly affect the decisions you make and what you do:

- Most people are willing to risk their lives before

they would risk their reputations.

- Safety is found in numbers. As human beings, we naturally despise being alone or ostracized.

- People dislike appearing silly. If leaders or "stronger" folks say you are wrong, they tend to follow what they think rather than sticking by their beliefs. This can easily land you right in the middle of "group thinking," which can be detrimental in crisis situations.

Mastering your emotions doesn't happen overnight. It literally only takes a millisecond to allow anger and/or fear to invade your mind. It takes dedicated time to develop the ability to hone in on emotions that tend to cloud your brain during stressful situations. But practicing the above things and being consciously aware of them can be the difference between life and death.

Rules of Survival Psychology

In order to have a better chance of surviving or even making the best of situations that are not considered as a crisis, there are things you can do to mentally extract yourself to avoid the scenario from getting worse than it already is:

- Learn the value of responding at the right time. If you need to act immediately, use all the information you have gathered to perform without hesitation. The information you get from being consciously aware will be your best friend.

- People who have a clear mind and respond fast

have a far better advantage in situations that require survival techniques.

- You have a better chance of surviving a crisis if you strive to do things correctly the first time around. You can do your absolute best when you are focused and calm so that you can hone in on what is required of you in a situation.

- Learn the value of making mistakes and learning from them. If you do something wrong, go back and look at things you could have done differently. Building upon improving will help you to make the best of all situations, bad *and* good.

- Take the time to quickly think of all the scenarios that could play out from your potential actions. Carefully calculate what might happen if you make a mistake, etc. At the same time, you need to have the mindset of moving forward and don't dwell on what you could have done differently.

- Don't let the possibility of failure prevent you from doing what you need to do to move forward and survive.

- In order to live through the most intense of crisis's, you must have the dedication to give 110% of your energy to the mission of survival.

Situational Awareness Skills

Now that you have read a few pointers on what it takes to wrap your mind around how to think like a spy, not it is time to discuss vital tips in order to keep yourself alive in drastic situations.

Situational awareness is formed from the ability to recognize, process, and comprehend vital aspects of information about what is occurring around you. There are many situations that could easily be prevented if more folks practiced situational awareness. It's all about being consciously aware of all the environmental elements paired with respect to time, the understanding of what things mean, and how their status changes after particular variables occur. Having this kind of awareness is made up of these key points:

- Being able to adequately observe time, smell, sound, and sight

- Comprehending the body language and behavior of those around you

- Memory, preparation, and practice

Confused? No worries. We will talk more about these key points below!

14

DANIEL BRAND

Adequately Observing with Your Senses

Being observant is the foundation that holds all the aspects of social awareness. While many people can see, they fail to pay attention to elements that have the potential to cause problems. Many people listen, but they actually fail to hear what is being said in-between the lines. We tend to hear what we want to hear.

The ability to control your mindset during crisis gives you the ultimate power in gaining control over a bad situation. It's not something that we are born with, but rather a skill that we must practice on a regular basis to be able to depend on it if we are faced with a combat-type scenario.

- **Sight**: Many of us avoid our peripheral vision, which allows important pieces of the puzzle to hide in the background. In the spy world, it's not only crucial to focus on what lies ahead, but what lies on the sidelines as well. Multitasking when it comes to what we see takes dedicated practice. While you focus on what is in front of you, learn to take mental notes on the things going on around you and right outside of your line of vision. This helps you to stay focused on what is ahead, yet notice pertinent things that are on your sides.

- Sound: Our ears, however, do not have the same capability as our eyes to multitask. But as you learn to consciously listen, you will be amazed at what you can hear is going on all around you. Practice is the only thing that can help to establish this habit. Learn to be consciously aware of the sounds around you. What do you think they are? If you are unsure, investigate, so in the future you know what that sound relates to.

- Smell: Even though human beings are not equipped with the same sense of smell as per say, a canine, it is a powerful tool that can help us remember things. It can trigger memories about distinct smells of people, certain foods, and help us detect the presence of dangerous situations, like a fire. Our sense of smell is literally a mental anchor that helps us to determine what to do or how to act in particular scenarios.

- Timing: Ah, the subject of time. How often are you late to obligations? How early do you leave your home or workplace to get to where you need to be on time? While distractions are lurking around every corner, learn to discipline yourself into noting how long it takes to get to point A to point B with various things such as weather and traffic. If you have a goal to be less of a target, this element is key in order to pay attention to all aspects that are occurring around you.

Comprehending Body Language

As a spy, you have a respect and a realization for how absolutely powerful the human brain is. Our minds are extremely complex contraptions controlled by an equally complex operator. Situational awareness is about actually learning how to understand signs, an important point being how to read people.

Our body does things naturally in accordance to stimulants from the environment. Knowing and understanding these reactions could literally mean the difference between life and death for not just you, but those surrounding you as well.

- **Personal space:** Everyone has their own personal bubble that is also known as their comfort zone. When you talk to someone, pay close attention to where their feet are positioned. If they are not content with being around you, they will probably take a step backward.

- **Eye contact:** Eye contact is a crucial part of conversing and reading other people. If you notice that people are looking down, away, or seem deep in thought when you are speaking to them, this means they are trying their best to avoid the conversation. When people are deeply focused on what you are saying, they will make constant eye contact with you and engage with you.

- **Tone of voice:** You can understand people's emotions and how they are feeling by simply paying attention to the tone they are speaking. This means that as a spy, you need to learn the importance of establishing a good rapport, as well as learn to listen and to influence skills. These are what help you to maintain control when conversing.

- **Behavior:** There are general actions that people do unconsciously that you should keen in on, such as talking too fast or slow, talking loudly, sweating profusely, shaking of hands, acting too smooth, etc. Paying attention to general actions, as well as all of the aspects above can help you determine a possible problem that may arise before it has the chance to accelerate. This could mean the difference between you getting yourself and others out of danger instead of becoming a victim.

Practice Makes Perfect

With all things, it takes practice to become good at it. Situational awareness is no different. This is one of those skills that you must have dedicated discipline to adequately develop.

- **Memory** is a key factor in perfecting situational awareness. Memory is one of those skills that you can only develop by exercising your brain with small tests and tasks. Our brain is a muscle, which needs to be used and strengthened just like any other muscle in our body. There are a few memory games you could partake in, such as:

- Get out a deck of cards and try to memorize cards in their order for as long as you can recall.

- When going to the store, take note of how many people are standing in front of you, even go as far as counting the amount of ladies to men.

- **Preparation** is all about being as ready as you can when a threat arises. We never know exactly how we are going to act and react to things that occur, but being mentally prepared is a good practice. It also means taking note of when to act before a situation could become worse. For example, if you know bad weather is headed your way, you are likely to stock up on staple items. If you are headed to a large event in the next week, you may make a plan to avoid commuting headaches by taking another route, etc.

The key to memory is based upon the creation of a mental anchor that is tied to what you can easily recall. By associating traits with things you are familiar with, your situational awareness skills will help you when crisis is in the shadows.

Using Situational Awareness in Dangerous Situations

From sexual assault to home invasions and mass shootings, life-threatening situations can happen at any time, without warning. The following is a scenario, followed by the crucial tips that could mean living through a traumatic experience.

Imagine yourself walking onto a bus, headed home after a night on the town. Next, one of the passengers takes a bag and throws it over your head, while another person ties your hands.

"Sit and stay, or we will shoot you. If you do what we say, you might see your family again."

Your heart is pounding, and your mind is racing, wondering what in the world to do next. Your conscience kicks in, as you are not the only human being on the bus. You gather from listening to the bad guys speaking to one another that a group of terrorists has taken the entire bus captive. You realize you only have a small amount of time to escape alive.

While it is never totally possible to guarantee you will never become a victim of a similar situation, there are things you can do to improve your chances of coming out of these predicaments alive.

Be aware of your surroundings

Even if you have massive training, if you don't stay in a conscious state of awareness, you are diminishing your chances of remaining safe. In military and police fields, they train their folks in uniform to use colors in order to classify a particular state of mind and keep yourself on a broad level of awareness.

Pay close attention to the norms of those surrounding you. Does it seem too quiet? Is a group of people wearing oddly heavy coats during warm weather? Matching the baseline of norms could help you spot danger before it occurs. This is why when you travel you should always conduct research as to what the social norms are for where you are headed to.

Pay Attention to Your Pace

It's highly unnatural to see someone that *wants* to go at the same speed as you. It's basic instinct to avoid walking in a similar stride as a stranger. Or to keep up the same speed on a car side by side. If there is an individual opting to match your pace, they are probably a suspect and someone to watch for. Speed up and slow down to see if they still try their best to catch up or match your pace. If they do, get away as soon and as quickly as possible.

Depend on Yourself

In touchy situations, the only person you can really trust and depend on is yourself. Even when resolving situations goes smoothly, emergency responders still take time to arrive. That means you cannot hope, pray, or expect that a Good Samaritan will come to your rescue. Reality is not like the movies. This is why being self-reliant is one of the most crucial things that will keep you alive. It's *not* selfish if you are ready to act to get yourself in a better position than those around you.

Stay in Motion

It's a natural reaction to freeze in crisis, but it's one of the worst things you can do in order to get yourself to safety. Movement is what saves lives. Think about it; those who survive a plane crash often die from inhaling too much smoke. Car crash victims are often engulfed in a fiery explosion because they didn't escape the car in time. Moving targets are a heck of a lot harder to hit with a gun or a knife than stationary ones. Taking action increases your chances of survival ten-fold!

Don't Play Nice

This is not giving you an excuse to not help someone in need, but a reminder that you should remain aware and discerning. Criminals are those that know how to take advantage of one's kind heart. Take for instance Ted Bundy, a serial killer who faked injuries to lure his victims. In a similar way, just because a seemingly nice person is holding a baby in their arms, does not automatically make them a good person.

Don't Try to Be the Hero

Even though you are reading this book to obtain the knowledge and skill set that it takes to become a spy, does not mean you *have* to use them. While the feeling of empowerment is great, remaining smart is better. Don't purposely put yourself in danger just to prove yourself.

Real Life Scenario: Putting It All Together

Now that you have learned some of the tips it takes to remain calm and survive crisis situations, it is time to put them all together in a real-life scenario. We are going to use the situation of an active shooter since these situations seem to be on the rise these days.

First, you should know that active shooters can target *everyone* in *any* place. They are defined as people who engage in killing or attempt to kill individuals that are populated and/or confined place. There's typically no straightforward pattern they follow to select those they kill. This makes these scenarios very unpredictable. This is why I have picked this type of scenario because so much happens before our good ole folks in blue have a chance to arrive at the scene. This will hopefully prepare you both physically and mentally to deal with an active shooter situation.

You are at a well-known concert hall watching your favorite band. During the high point of a song, you hear a gunshot coming somewhere from the seats at the top of the building. In the corner of your eye, you saw a man go down and the crowd starts to panic and run like chickens with their heads cut off. What do you do?

First, you need to look for possible dangers. At events like concerts, it's probably dark in many areas and hard to see. Since there are shots being fired, get down low but stay where you have a vantage point of the potential shooters. Also, gather where the nearest exits are located.

If you have managed to find an escape route, follow these steps:

- Create a plan in mind. Which exit would be the most efficient to head to?

- Do not wait for others to follow your lead. Escape if and when you are able.

- If you have a bunch of stuff with you, leave it behind. Belongings can be replaced, your life cannot. I would suggest not leaving your phone behind, so you can get a hold of loved ones and those you were with if you are separated.

- If you can, assist others in escaping.

- Do not attempt to move those that have been wounded.

- When law enforcement arrives, follow their instructions.

- If you deem it necessary, call 911 when you have gotten to a safe location.

   If you are unable to locate a path to escape:

- Find a place to hide that the shooter(s) cannot easily access you, such as:

- Anywhere out of the view of the shooter

- An office/room with a locking door. Blockade the door with furniture if there is any.

- A place that will not restrict possibility for movement

   If you are left with very little options, and if your life is in immediate danger, you can incapacitate the shooter by doing the following:

- Yelling to distract them

- Throwing items at them or creating improvised weapons to protect yourself

- Being and acting aggressive/charging at the shooter

Home Security Skills

Being a spy is realizing and not avoiding the fact that today's technology provides ease of access to your personal life by the wrong hands. Having a secure home is one of the foundational steps to becoming a trustworthy, adequate agent.

Physically Securing Your Home

Many people use the dark of night as a cloak to take advantage of folks who do not take home security seriously. There a plethora of things you can do to make your home less attractive to potential snoopers.

- **Fake it till you make it**: This is one of the cheapest yet most beneficial ways to secure your home from bad peeps.

- Give the illusion that you have a dog by purchasing "Beware of Dog" signs, dog toys, food, and water bowls. If a stranger comes to your door, act as if you are putting your dog into the other room before letting them in.

- Buy and install fake security cameras. This will keep criminals from wanting to get caught doing anything naughty on your property. The best part? They are only around 5 bucks!

- **Trim your bushes/shrubs often:** By keeping your shrubs and other outdoor plants untrimmed, you are freely giving potential perpetrators cover to hide.

- **Light it up**: Where there are lights, there are bound to be less bad people lurking around. Get motion censored lights for both the back and front of your home.

- **Keep it alive:** People are less likely to break into places that looked lived in or look to have people at home.

- If you are planning a trip or an extended stay away, rotating lights are a good investment.

- Stop by your local post office and hold your mail till you are back.

- Reschedule deliveries that are to be expected

- Have friends or neighbors come by to water plants, take care of the house, feed/walk pets, etc.

- **Lock it up:** It's easy to bust down a hollow door, so opt for solid ones. Also, don't just get flimsy locks that are easy to pick or break. Opt for burglar resistant glass and hinge pins. You may also want to spend the money to get a deadbolt for each exterior door that is high quality.

- **Home security and surveillance:** A solid peace of mind for anyone, including operatives, comes from knowing that their home is protected by security and video technology when they are not present to see things unravel. There are a variety of security systems that can easily fit into many budgets. And with today's technology, it's now not unheard of for folks to have monitoring capabilities in their homes as well. These are typically activated by a motion sensor and can even be watched from a mobile device.

Secret Security

In order to keep your home safe, you must take the time to think like an intruder when you are prepping your home. This means that the leaving the spare key under the doormat trick or leaving the television on is probably not going to cut it anymore. Burglars have become just as sophisticated as anyone else, if not more.

That being said, there are some easy methods to securing your home in more advanced ways that are much harder to detect by a professional criminal. The best way to go about this is to get inside the mind of an intruder and think how you would case your own place.

- Burglars are always looking for easy routes to access quickly. This means you should look into replacing or installing window latches, door locks, peepholes, etc. Also, remove your unit number from your door keys.

- Install doors that are sturdy and equipped with strong bolts.

- Install bright light bulbs that light up hiding places.

- Lock the apartment fire escape ladder so that this is one less place for a criminal to enter and escape.

- Purchase an intruder alarm system.

Thinking outside the box is another great way to detour burglars if they do manage to make it into your home. Many people keep their precious belongings stored in places that are easily accessible or quite obvious. Instead, opt for hiding your precious mementos and belongings in these unique places:

- Place valuable things in:

- Thick books

- Empty cans, such as hair spray or Pringle cans

- Unutilized electronics like game consoles and stereos.

- Placed in a baggie inserted in vegetables

When it comes to proofing your home not just from ordinary people but from other professional spies like you, a surveillance system of some kind if a must. But there is a catch; you need to utilize that unique out-of-the-box train of thought in order to place these types of gadgets in areas that people will not think to look, so they have no idea they are being detected. This means that you should not overlook everyday things. Install surveillance within a television, a clock, a plant, etc. Or place it on a bookshelf, lamp, nightstand, clothing, etc.

Keeping Your Identity Secure within Your Home

A major concept of being a spy is the ability to keep your spy whereabouts and missions undercover. This means that there are some necessary things you will have to do to conduct yourself in a spy manner in order to keep your identity safe.

- **Utilize virtual credit card numbers**: To be able to keep your identity out of bad hands, you must learn the importance of using disposable *everything*. If you are concerned that your identity and safety could be compromised while online shopping or sleuthing, use virtual credit card numbers. You will have to call around, for not all banks have this option. But it is a good one to have, for it allows you to use single-use credit card numbers to isolate transactions and prevent fraud.

- **Encrypt sensitive data:** Most real-life spies typically don't have personal data to encrypt, since it's been sacrificed for secrecy. But as a regular person, you should invest in a nifty encryption tool to hide sensitive data that bad guys can use for all the wrong reason.

- **Modifying printer to print secret messages:** Did you know you can print invisible messages through a regular ole printer? All you have to do is modify the printer to use concentrated lemon juice in the place of yellow ink! Those messages can then be discovered by exposing the document to heat.

- **Lock digital devices:** All the devices you use every day have the ability to create a trail of where they have been. For a spy, that information can be accessed way too easily. If you do not have a plan to encrypt that information, you should at least make it a practice to lock all of these things down. It's a nice peace of mind knowing that your devices are secured. While it may seem annoying, you will thank yourself when someone tries to breach your information to only get slapped on the hand by the security you installed!

- **Browse the web securely:** The internet is another one of those technologies than can be easily tracked by peeping eyes, which is by no means a good thing for a spy of any degree. It's a good idea to install a buddy called Tor so that you can browse the internet anonymously. If you are communicating directly with your home base, it would be an even better idea to use a VPN service to encrypt your activities online.

- **Hide files within other files:** One of the best hiding techniques spies utilize is known as *steganography*, which is the art of hiding things in plain sight. This tactic can be highly useful, even in your own personal life. It's all about making things secure through obscurity. So in the matter of hiding files, you can put them within other files, so that when someone comes across it, they don't have the urge to click it, since its hiding in plain sight. Learn how to do it here (http://lifehacker.com/5831270/learn-how-to-hide-things-in-plain-sight-with-the-secret-hiding-places-manual?tag=security)!

- **Create devices into alarm systems:** Luckily for you, almost all devices nowadays have the capability to be an alarm system. For just a buck you can make your laptop into a sounding alarm, same with iPhones and other smartphone devices. Almost all laptops have free programs people can download so that their webcam can be a security camera.

- **Hide messages in audio files:** As you have read previously, there are a variety of ways to tuck away messages and codes within plain sight. But this one is quite unique. With a simple download of a couple pieces of software, there is hardly any effort in having to encode secret text and images within audio files. If you want to check it out, look at the tutorial here (http://lifehacker.com/5807289/how-to-hide-secret-messages-and-codes-in-audio-files)!

- **Create a portable privacy toolkit from a flash drive:** When you are out on missions, you will more than likely need access to the internet to search things, but you do not want your information tracked and hacked to give someone the ability to locate you. This is why one of these handy dandy kits made from a regular ole flash drive is needed! It can keep your internet activity safe, along with your passwords, email, and web browser content under wraps. Look at this tutorial here (https://lifehacker.com/5629082/without-a-trace-turn-your-flash-drive-into-a-portable-privacy-toolkit) on how to create one.

- **Disappear:** As a last resort, if your identity has been compromised or if you feel your efforts from the steps above have gone to waste, you can disappear by stealing (yes, stealing) the identity of a deceased individual. While it sounds ludicrous, it is a solid way from becoming a victim of identity theft. You can learn how to nab the identity of deceased person here (https://lifehacker.com/5822345/how-to-steal-a-dead-persons-identity).

Travel Safety Skills

Traveling the world, while a fun, can also be detrimental. Even for the average person, personal things like wallets can be lost, which hold tons of information that when falling into the hands of the wrong people, can cost you your identity. So, as a spy, there are things that you have to do in order to take that extra step of necessary precaution as you travel the world on missions or just for pleasure. Most of these tips are for those that plan to travel abroad and will give you a peace of mind when it comes to visiting places you may not be familiar with.

Conduct research before traveling

Thanks to the invention and expansion of the internet, we can easily look up information about the destinations we plan to visit from the comfort of our laptop computers and other mobile devices. Take advantage of this resource and do your homework before heading to your mission's destination.

As we are all too aware, all things are not created equal. It's recommended to visit sites like

SmarTraveller.gov.au to not only become familiarized with the destination but to become informed of security threats, important phone numbers in case of emergency and more.

Skip the social media posts

Even though traveling is exciting and you have the urge to share with family and friends via social media, opt not to. I know, easier said than done. But posting the dates of a potential trip can easily be seen by a criminal who can mark on their calendar to make a one-stop shopping spree out of your unoccupied home.

While there are security settings on almost all media platforms, don't be fooled into thinking this will keep all of your information safe. So often we see folks post the exact time, place, destination, hotel, flight, and etc. that they will be on. By doing this, you are literally laying the groundwork out for bad people to take advantage of you. In fact, criminals browse the internet often in search of their next careless victim. Don't put yourself at risk.

Ask for an extra key and a higher floor at the hotel

Even the most seasoned spies are humbled enough to know that they could be being followed or tracked at any given time, no matter how much of their efforts went into going undercover or remaining anonymous. If you are traveling alone, it is a good idea to ask for an additional room key. This will give others around you the impression that the other key is for a friend or spouse tagging along. Also, it's a fact that crimes tend to occur on the lowest floors of hotels, so ask for a room on the third floor or even higher.

Don't utilize the safe at the hotel

While the convenience of a "safe place" to store your stuff is a nice hotel accommodation, they are not the best quality. Besides the fact, anyone that works at the hotel can easily bypass the code and unlock any safe in any room. Another good tip is always making it a habit of carrying your passport with you, especially in countries you are unfamiliar with. Why? Because you may come across a situation where the government may ask to see it. If you leave it sitting in the 'not so safe' hotel safe, you will be in quite a bad position.

Purchase a doorstopper alarm

Getting yourself one of these nifty gadgets and making sure to add it to your suitcase of belongings when you travel is a must. Doorstoppers alarm by simply wedging them beneath your hotel door while you relax or sleep. If anyone attempts to come into a room that is not expected, it sounds a loud alarm, alerting the occupant inside.

Out-scam, the scammers

Scammers, unfortunately, do some of their best work as folks like you travel. As you travel about your merry way, always be wary of folks that don't have the best of intentions. Among almost all crowds you venture into is a travel scammer, and they are darn good at what they do. Especially as a spy, be prepared by knowing the typical scams that scammers use to get information from people. More often than not these days, the consequences of being too naïve can result in way worse than having your wallet stolen.

Stop the wallet trick

While we are on the subject of wallets, please do yourself a favor and don't participate in the "hanging hidden wallet" trick. There are so many tourists that strap their wallets around their necks. But in reality, where you hide your wallet is really not that hidden and there are many times its easily visible. Plus, it's such a travel cliché nowadays to have things hidden in your body that scammers and traveling bad guys know what to look for. If anything, opt for purchasing a wallet that has RFID protection to protect anyone from scooping up your credit card information.

Digitize important documents

Thank goodness for the world of technology! Not only does it allow us to make more room in our bags, but it enables us to carry documents that we don't want snooping eyes to see.

When you travel, especially as a spy, copy and download pictures of your consulate and embassy numbers, travel confirmations, in-case-of-emergency contacts, flight details, travel insurance information, passport, and driver's license onto a flash drive. Carrying all this important personal documentation of the convenience of a flash drive makes it less likely to be snagged from you as you go about your missions. Plus, it's a lot harder for you to lose.

Act like a local

It's best to prevent yourself from standing out in areas you are not familiar with by learning to blend in with the people where you are visiting. This does not only mean avoiding wearing extremely bright clothing, but to actually become part of the landscape of people by wearing what the natives wear, learning their customs, know the culture, walking with confidence and taking note of transportation options. As a spy, you want to make it very difficult to track you online and physically amongst a crowd as well.

Only taxi from trustworthy sources

While the creation of Lyft, Uber, and Airbnb have been sweeping the world, they are not the most trustworthy lines of transportation. Be sure to use extra caution and an extra dose of judgment when you opt for car riding services. Or, just skip them altogether and utilize public transportation or reputable taxi services in the area. It's not to say that bad things will not happen, but you are more likely to get help if needed in public transit or within more reputable lines of travel.

Social Engineering Skills

Another main aspect of successful spying and being consciously aware of your surroundings is by taking the time to read the vibe from the people you are surrounded by. Analyzing human beings is a crucial piece of the job of a spy, for the underlying actions and non-verbal words of people usually are holding the most important information.

As an observant, it is practically in your job title to be able to have the capability of getting to know people better than they even know themselves. This is the only way to get the most pertinent information from them in a short amount of time. This chapter will outline a few key areas of getting to know people, as well as realizing when they are being dishonest with you and attempting to lead you down the wrong path to throw you off.

How to Get to Really Know Personality

There are many factors as we dive into the nitty-gritty of getting to truly know the personality of another human being. From body language, preferences in color and the choices one makes, these are just a few of the main factors that can lead us to gathering the necessary information into the personality traits of a person. There is no "perfect map" into getting the picture right 100%, but knowing some of the inner workings can indeed help you to analyze another person's personality.

To truly understand the personal characteristics of another human being, you must become seasoned in a bit of psychology. The behaviors of a person may seem either totally odd or completely meaningless when seen by itself, but it can be of great significance when it all comes together with the remaining actions a person does.

Putting Together the Past with Personality

To really get aspects of a person's true personality accurate, you must get to know a little about them and their past. How did this individual grow up? How were they treated as a child? What were their relationships like with parents and siblings? For example, you will see that the youngest sibling in the family may become extremely ambitious as a result of being the weakest kid. They feed off ambition because this makes them feel more powerful or as powerful as the oldest sibling. After knowing such a tiny fact, many other things become clearer, such as why this particular person may want to become a millionaire, etc. This does not mean that every young kid will grow up to have an ambitious side, however. This is just a prime example to prove that knowing a bit about someone's past can be a precursor to their actions in the now.

Ways to Know Personality through Social Media Posts

The world today would be seemingly obsolete to many without the utilization of technology and social networking. That being said, there is a lot to be said about what people post on their social media profiles that you can decipher and get many personality clues from.

In order to analyze someone's personality via the assistance of their social media, you will need a sample of posts. Moods change and vary all the time, which can make it difficult to form a good, solid conclusion about the individual whose posts you are looking at. You will have to do a bit of working connecting different posts together to find common things. While not all common posts should say the same thing, they should be pointing in a particular direction, in which then you can confidently come to a conclusion about that person via their posts. Also, photos and videos can share a wide variety of crucial information as well!

Interpreting Body Language

We spend our lives figuring out how to decipher other individuals' nonverbal prompts. While we're caught up with attempting to unravel their messages, they are additionally attempting to disentangle our own. There are times when you need other individuals to know precisely how you're feeling, particularly when those sentiments are both positive and responded. This isn't generally simple to do, particularly in case you're not an especially emotive sort of individual. At different circumstances, in any case, you certainly need to conceal your inward sentiments. To keep away from passionate spillage, you may need to work doubly hard. Contingent upon the circumstance, you may need to put on your Lady Gaga-style poker face.

Non-verbal communication is quite literally the dialect of the body. You may surmise that you just demonstrate your feelings through your face. However, that is truly just the tip of the iceberg. Your whole body partakes in the matter of either appearing or concealing your mental state. To control that show implies you need to control your body's oblivious prompts. This guide will demonstrate to you how, beginning starting from the top. When you're set, you'll have a substantially more prominent comprehension of seemingly insignificant bodily gestures that can give those that actually pay attention signals that give way to what someone might actually be thinking and feeling. We will work our way from the tippy-top of our heads all the way down to our toes!

The Head

When I said we were going to begin at the very top of the head, I meant just that! Your scalp, otherwise known as your hair, can tell others a lot about your mental and emotional state of mind. People have good and bad hair days, but sometimes that should not be overlooked so easily. When one is stressed, perhaps they forget to brush out their lovely locks. At a single glance, one may take notice that you may not be completely together at that moment. Or, having bed head may make one assume that you have a sexy night on the town the night before. No matter the cut, style or color of your hair, having a groomed appearance tells others that you are in control of the way your day is turning out. If you do not have hair, that problem may be solved, but it also leaves your brows to question. They can give away cues such as excessive frowning which is a pretense as to how you might be feeling.

Your other permanent features of your face cannot be changed (unless you go under the knife and receive plastic surgery!) but they can prominently display and give away cues as to what you are experiencing and going through to others. The smallest movements that our faces make can give away a lot of what we are thinking to others. These are known by psychologists as "micro-expressions." These are vital in truly interpreting bodily language because they can lead to a contradiction of what someone might be saying, which leads one to believe that what is coming out of someone's mouth might not be as truthful as it sounds. For example, if you are attracted to someone and wish to impress them, you may have those butterflies within you that you think you are hiding well. But the slightest pulling of the muscles in such areas like the mouth shows that you are panicking a bit on the inside. Take a moment to grimace for a second. Take note of how your entire face feels when you do so. There are many micro expressions that people protrude from the outside when they are afraid, lying, etc. If you wish to be dishonest for good reasons, learn how to control these facial muscles, for they will give you away quicker than your white lie will.

Your eyes are also a big source of non-verbal communication. When learning how to communicate with people more openly and thoroughly, you need to learn about the balance of looking and staring, for there is a fine line. Too much looking into someone else's eyes can cause discomfort in the other person, while too little can make you seem uninterested. This includes eye gestures such as eye rolls, etc. A twinkle of the eye can make others around you feel at ease, do not underestimate the power of a smirk or smile!

The chin and neck are not to be forgotten either! While they are both facial features we are born with and cannot change, if you are constantly jutting your chin out in front of you, people may read you and assume you obstinate. The neck has the ability to be flexible and is not a fixed area of the body. But the way you hold your head up can say a lot about you as a person and also what you might be thinking or feeling at any certain time. If you choose to hold your head straight up, you will appear confident. If your eyes are always scanning the floor, the opposite will seem true.

The Torso

If you hold your neck up nice and straight, then your torso will follow this action and align right along with it. Confidence will show if you keep your shoulders and back straight and not hunching forward. If you rather choose to sag more around the torso, perhaps you are trying to gain the attention of someone who is sympathetic. Chronic sagging in the torso area tells others that you may not feel good physically or mentally or that you are very unconfident in yourself. Keeping yourself in a solid upright position has more good effects than non-verbally informing people you are confident in yourself. Always allowing your torso area of the body to sag will lead to a variety of pesky health problems later on. So sit up straight!

The Arms and Hands

Your upper limbs give way to perhaps the most essential and most easy to read tools of the human body when it comes to accurately reading bodily languages. They can non-verbally communicate a lot of things, including things you wish not to inform others around you of. Excessive hand fidgeting can portray boredom or anxiety. Tightly crossing your arms may make you seem like you are angry. Arrogant mannerisms like placing your arms akimbo may be unintentional, but other people highly read into those sorts of mannerisms. It is important if you do not want to give yourself away *too* much that you learn to neutrally keep your hands and arms from giving away impressions that are actually not true to you. The most recommended way to keep your hands and arms is to hold them in your lap. When you are standing, keep them at your sides or in another resting place that is comfortable for you so that it does not look forced to other people.

The Legs

The lower limbs of your body give away just as much as your upper extremities do. If you tightly cross your legs, this may create a "closed off" view

47

to other people. But splaying them out makes you seem too carefree and careless. In order to create a comfortable, relaxed and open-minded feel to others you need to be relaxed but not so much so that it seems like you are bored with the situation at hand. What we wear can make differences in this, however. Obviously, women who wear skirts will have to keep their legs closed tighter than if they are wearing pants. This is why it is stressed to not wear too short of skirts or other clothing that makes you feel uncomfortable in your own skin. The anxiety of trying to look good in articles of clothing that you otherwise do not feel your best in *will* show to others.

Anxious feelings can also present themselves physically through the means of excessive leg shaking and foot tapping. People who come off jittery may just want to burn off a few excess calories, but more than likely they feel anxious about the situation around them or about something that may be on their mind. The legs make up the biggest part of the human body, so even with the smallest movements, people take notice. Instead of shaking your legs, be conscious of other ways you can prevent this. To help the bodily jitters, make it a habit, even in scenarios that aren't the most comfortable, to sit with your legs gently crossed and your hands nicely folded in your lap. Not only will other people take notice of how calm you seem, but it will help you to settle feelings of anxiousness as well.

The Feet

If you are someone that shakes their legs, then

you inevitably are going to shake your feet simultaneously as well. There is also the tapping of toes, which can indicate to others that you might be in a rush or anxious to get going. Tapping of the feet also may be used to gain the attention of another person if you do not want to come off as rude if you say something. Toe tapping is typically a body language that is used when someone feels pressured for time and does not want to rudely engage in conversation, even if it would get the ball rolling faster. But in reality, these people may be seen as rude anyways or just plain annoying with all that tapping!

Did you know that your feet can also communicate to others of fearful feelings and confidence? It is all about the way you move from point A to point B. If you walk in a stride that is straight and strong, you come across as someone that people can depend on. Good posture of any sort portrays confidence to others. Slouching and slumping, however, portray a lack of confidence or ever a fear of where you might be going. You give off cues unconsciously by being either fearful or confident in your destination. Also, if someone wants or is interested in engaging with you, their feet will point right towards you. If their feet are pointing away from you, their minds are on another topic and it is a sign they would either rather be somewhere else or may be in a slight hurry and have another place to be at the time.

A Few Tricks in Reading Body Language

As you have read so far in this chapter, the

ability to read the body language of others can give us a lot of information about those around us. If you feel like you will never be good at reading body language, chin up! We as human beings actually pick up on more bodily cues than we realize. Only 7% of communication is what comes from verbal speaking while 38% comes from just the tone of our voices and 55% comes from non-verbal body language. Learning to become aware of that much bigger percent can give you an edge over others and even pave your way to success! So, next time you are in a meeting, on a date, having fun with your kids or hanging out with friends, watch for the following cues:

- **Crossed arms and legs** – This action portrays possible resistance to your ideas or the thoughts of others. The arms and legs are physical barricades that suggest that they may not be quite as open as to what you are saying, even if they happen to have a smile of their face and seem quite intrigued by what is spewing from your mouth. If someone's arms and legs are crossed, it is a pretty telling sign that they are blocked off from everything in front of them, mentally and emotionally. While it may not be intentional, it is still very revealing of the way they think and feel.

- **Smile with crinkled eyes** – When you view the smile of others, a smile can lie through anything, but the sparkle in the eye and the creases a true smile makes around the eyes can't. Smiles that are genuine reach all the way up to the eyes. People often smile to hide their feelings and thoughts. So the next time you see someone smile at you, do not take as much notice in their pearly whites, but rather the crinkles that are created by the smile at the corner of the eyes. If they are non-existent, they are using the smile as a shield to hide something.

- **The copying of your body language** – While this sounds like a child-like game, the mirroring of body language is how we tend to bond with people in an unconscious manner. In social environments as you engage, does that person cross their legs when you do? Do they cock their heads in the same way you do when conversing with others? The copying of body language is actually a sign that the conversation itself is going great and that the other people are being quite receptive to what you are saying. This is useful when it comes to negotiating, for it shows you actual proof that the opposing party is considering your deal.

- **Posture creates a story** – Think about a person of power in your life, whether in the workplace or elsewhere. Take note of their posture. More than likely these individuals will walk into a room with an erect posture, palms facing down and communicate non-verbally with open gestures. Posture is critical in providing a story to others about your life. Standing straight with shoulders back portrays a position of power. While slouching portrays less power. Maintaining a decent posture tells others that you command to be respected and promotes engagement to others, whether or not you are a leader.

- **Lying eyes** – I am sure most of you remember the phrase of "look at me in the eye when I am speaking to you." Growing up, we were taught that avoiding eye contact was a perfect sign of lying. But that is common knowledge, so many people lie to one another even while maintaining perfect eye contact. That is why those that are being dishonest tend to overcompensate eye contact, giving it to others to the point of discomfort. Seven to ten seconds is the average that people hold eye contact for, longer when they are listening rather than speaking. If you come into contact with someone whose eye contact makes you uncomfortable, especially someone who doesn't bother to blink, they are more than likely being dishonest with you.

- **Discomfort in the brows** – There are a few main emotions that our eyebrows portray: fear, worry, and surprise. It is impossible to have raised eyebrows and attempting to have a casual conversation. If you are talking about something that shouldn't be causing any eyebrows to raise, something else is going on around you or with that person internally.

- **Excessive nodding** – If you are speaking to someone and they are constantly nodding their head, this may signal that they are concerned about your thoughts or they may doubt your ability to follow through with something.

- **Clenched jaw** – Clenched jaws, tightening of the neck and a furrowed brow are all tell-tale signs of stress. It doesn't matter what is coming from a person's mouth, if any of these signs are noticeable, they are hiding their anxiety, stress, and discomfort. Perhaps a conversation is leading down a path of something they are not comfortable speaking about. They key here is to take note of any mismatches of what the person is saying and then what their body language is telling you.

These will help you to know what another individual is feeling, especially if you are looking to decode them via their body language alone. Notice the way they either provide you with good or bad eye contact. Look down from time to time, are their feet facing you? There are tiny ways to diagnose bodily language and how one truly feels in various scenarios. Like every great skill, practice makes perfect. As you learn the once mysterious ways of body language, ask a friend or family member if you could practice reading their language. The body both consciously and unconsciously reflects the mental state we are in. As you learn and become more seasoned in reading people, you may start to notice things you can change to come off more calm and relaxed to others. This helps quite a bit in the world of dating. You do not want a stranger on a first date to feel on edge because you seem on edge physically. Learning to control your bodily cues in social environments is key to many things, including getting a step or two ahead in this dog-eat-dog world. While it is not yet possible to actually read a person's exact thoughts, you can learn a lot if not just enough from non-verbal body language.

The Basics of Profiling

In order to analyze people in a thorough, concise manner, one must learn the psychology of why people act the way they do and becoming seasoned with profiling people can help you to master this ability. It is important to pause the world around you and take the time to observe the actions and words of other people. While travel is meant to get to Point A to Point B, have you ever stopped to look further into the details of the hustle and bustle of an average traveler? In order to analyze people, you must be willing to see *beyond* what see!

Viewing People as Onions

While this may sound funny, a person's entire being should be visualized like the four layers of an onion. The deeper you get into the onion, the more you are able to determine how much you can really read into someone.

- *Skin* – Without being consciously aware of it, we tend to reveal more about ourselves to other people than we realize through personalities and traits.

- *Second layer* – This layer is often seen by people we have gotten to know better and who we appreciate in our lives, like co-workers and classmates. Since there is a sense of comfort and trust built between, people are able to comprehend one another on a basic level here.

- *Third layer* – This is a layer seen by best friends and other people we form close bonds with. There is a "locked" sense of trust and security with people that know you at this layer. We share secrets, pronounce concerns and other similar things.

- *Core* – Each and every person as a core. This is where secrets and thoughts are stored that are not shared with anyone but oneself. This layer is quite psychological.

Elimination of Barriers and Personal Prejudice

In order to really analyze others, you must be willing to tear down the barriers that you think are the truth about yourself and others. You must at times force yourself to believe and come to conclusions that you otherwise would not have. We are whisked away into scenarios that leave us feeling guilty and insecure, which blinds us into accepting the reality of things. Prejudice in the world of psychology goes way beyond just race and gender. You must acknowledge that prejudice is all about basing thoughts and opinions on ideas without facts. It is crucial to keep yourself in a neutral state of mind before getting consumed by false statements.

Test on Someone You Already Know

It is important when you are just beginning to start profiling people that you veer away from strangers. In order to really understand people, you do not know you will have to observe them for a period of time. This is why choosing a significant other, friend or co-worker is best to get your feet wet.

It is crucial to understand and recognize the "baseline profile" of the person you will be practicing on. This state is when the person is the most comfortable or at ease. Then, you can move on to observing their behaviors at random times. It may be a good idea to have a notebook with you at first, to jot down how the person you are observing behaves during different activities, days and how they interact with others.

Once you have gathered enough notes over a period of time of observation, you can now start to shape a list of patterns and common traits from the person's actions. Doing this creates a foundation to start building the truth of that person.

• Body language

• Facial expressions

• Eye movements

• Varying vocal tones

Then, it is time to jot out a list of unexpected behaviors, moments and other ticks that do not seem to fit into the "baseline" profile of the person you are observing.

Enhancing Your Knowledge

Now that you have gained some practice, it is time to profile someone you do not know or someone you wish to know better.

Define who they are – Allow their styles, appearance, and personality come out to "become them."

Recognize their vocalization towards a variety of people – Those that have a soft tone in their voice might signify that they are shy individuals, but you must also take note of the environment in which they are placed in as well. Louder tones of voice may signal that they feel the need to feel "higher" than those around them or like to be in command and in charge of other people. Does their voice change when defending an opinion? Do they communicate in an immature or mature way? Ensure that you are doing a good job of correctly deciphering between conversational exaggerations, slang, sarcasm, etc. Pay attention to the context of words and how that person allows them to flow as they talk as well.

Look at Eye Movements

Does the person you are observing tend to look straight into the eyes of others or off to the side or down to the ground? Do their eyes turn big when they are asked to provide an honest answer?

Evaluate their Self-Composure

Many people tend to be nervous when put into crowded areas and like to think of ways they can avoid going or being there. Those that are impatient in nature tap their feet more than calm people. Look for fidgeting, such as sighing, or looking at their phone. Watch for lip biting as well.

Tips and Tricks to Become a Better Analyzer

The best part of becoming an analyzer is that you do not have to go to a fancy FBI school in order to get into the minds of what people are thinking and feeling. People give off signals all the time, we just are typically blind to them unless we take the time to become educated on the tiniest of movements. It is all about knowing just what to look for in order to come to a conclusion about someone and crack their code. While there are no surefire methods to decipher what someone may be thinking, here are some surefire tips to ensure you are getting the full story from the pasts, presents, and futures of possible criminals or those that are withholding valuable intel.

• Begin with baseline reading. This will help you to establish a person's little quirks and so forth. A common way to do this is to give yourself time to observe a person's habits. This takes patience because some people are pretty hard to read. Even if you think a habit is not worth noting, note it anyways. Once you look back at your notes, even the little movements, habits or other actions that person took that seemed unessential at the time can pull many other notes you have jotted down together.

• Be aware of inconsistencies in a person's baseline personality versus gestures, words, and actions that do not quite fit in. This will help you to shape an overall personality profile over time.

- Ask specific, not vague questions. Open-ended inquiries do not work in truly reading anyone. Vague questions offer an opportunity to ramble in order for them to answer it, which makes it much more difficult to detect any sort of dishonesty. Ask questions that require people to provide you with a straight answer, but do not be too intrusive. Simple ask away, sit back and observe without interruption. This is where you will find that you receive your best inside information on this specific person.

- As you have learned, always be wary of a person's choice of words. They provide great insight into what a person is really trying to convey.

- Pay attention how a person leans. If their torso is facing away from you, this may indicate that this person is feeling stressed. It can also mean that they have much more on their mind than what you are attempting to say to soak into their minds.

- Gestures, like rubbing of the palms, touching and/or rubbing the forehead or rubbing palms against one's thigh highly, indicates that this individual is feeling rather stressed.

- Watch how people tend to stall. If you are observing and notice someone that closes their eyes longer than it takes for a simple blink, take time to clear their throat or asks you to repeat questions or what you have verbalized, they are taking time to stall to avoid something.

- Excessive blinking, fidgeting and a lack of eye contact are all tell-tale signs that someone is lying. However, these can be precursors to someone who may feel anxious about a situation as well. It is common for those that are lying through their teeth to look at those they speak with straight in the eyes. This can also signify that they are attempting to deceit you.

- Other depictions of someone being dishonest are the utilization of vagueness in extremely descriptive formats or a quivering voice.

- Eyes are not only a window to the soul. Excessive squinting and the constriction of the pupils may mean that this person may be bothered by what they are viewing.

- To improve detection of lies, take the time to observe children and how they act when they tell a white lie. We as adults typically learn to tell white lies in order to survive in social environments, but children have yet to learn this prominent skill. They are bad at being dishonest, which gives those that are practicing their beginning analyzing skills a great place to start observing actions when lying. One must keep in mind that some adults are much better at lying than others. Those that are not so good at it will show similar signs to that of dishonest children.

Self-Defense Skills

Did you know that when a person is exposed to a stressful situation, that they are likely to lose 50 percent of their fine motor skills and IQ? That's quite a bit, and too much when these are crucial things you need in order to survive. This is why training yourself for crisis can trigger your muscle memory to take over.

While there is always the option to hit a perpetrator in sensitive areas such as the pelvis, kidneys, ribs, neck, sinuses, or eyes, we are going to discuss what one can do to escape specific ways you are being bound, caged, attacked, grabbed, etc.

Bound with duct tape

A good first rule of thumb is to remember to consciously keep your elbows together as you are being tied up with duct tape. This will help you to get out of this binding later.

- If you are **able** to move your arms around:

- Lift your hands over your head.

- With a quick, strong movement, forcefully bring your hands down to your hips, aiming each of your wrists to each of your hips. The momentum of this movement should tear the tape.

* If you are **unable** to move your arms:

* Look for something in the vicinity that has a 90-degree angle, like a corncr, table, window sill, etc.

* Get close to the object and situate the tape against it, between your wrists and parallel to your arms.

* Quickly, move your hands up and down in a sawing motion as you push in on the edge. This angle acts as a knife, cutting the tape.

* If bound to a chair or other object:

* Lean forward towards your toes. Duct tape can only hold so much weight. The act of forcefully leaning will stretch and break the tape.

BOUND WITH ROPE

When your captor is tying your hands, make an effort to keep your elbows apart at your sides but the palms of your hands touching.

Lift your arms so that they are in front of you. Your hands should now be open, laying flat against each other and your elbows should be together.

Move your hands back and forth, like you are rubbing them together. The rope should eventually become loose and fall off.

When you are kidnapped

Criminal Minds doesn't lie; the first 24 hours of being forced into the hands of a bad person is the most crucial. During this time, you are at your strongest, which means you have a greater chance of escaping before becoming dehydrated or starved. It also means you are closer to the location at which you were nabbed.

As you plan your escape, be submissive and try to not look too much at your captors. Any kinds of aggressive behavior can provoke them to hurt you or make them suspicious that you are planning to run, which could whisk your chance of escaping away.

If you are attacked from behind

While the instinct you get when you are nabbed from behind is to lean forward, don't do this. Rather, create space between you and the assailant by stepping backward to throw them off balance. Your weight is your biggest asset in this situation. Once you get free, run and protect yourself with blows to sensitive areas.

If you are locked inside a vehicle

Look to see if there is something within reach to smash a window with. Aim for the corner of the window, since that is where glass is tighter and much easier to break. Most likely, you will not shatter a window with one hit. Keep hitting in the same area till you are successful.

When you are grabbed by an assailant

Find the captor's pinky finger and pull it back with all the power you got. This will help you to loosen their grip on you. Even the biggest, strongest individuals will let go if you yank their tiniest finger hard enough.

In the case, you are being followed

While it might take some guts to do so, make eye contact with the person following you. Turn towards them and yell "What?!" By simply letting the individual know that you are on to them, it will likely make them leave. Folks with ill intentions desire victims that are easy to catch off-guard.

If you can, opt to take left turns instead of right. Humans instinctively take right turns rather than left. This can detour the assailant. Also, look for places you can get to that are high, such as buildings or trees. Pursuers are not likely to go above ground level. Just keep in mind to actively search for an escape route in whatever place you are in.

Escape and Evade Skills

As a spy, expect there to be times where you land yourself unexpectedly in some trouble. Whether it is someone close on your tail attempting to uncover your true identity, or you need to escape quickly, this chapter will provide some pointers to help you get out of situations that can lead to entrapment and the possibility of all your hard work going straight to the trash.

Tips to Outlast Any Chase

Just because you are being hunted, does not mean you have to accept being the prey. Here are some go-to spy tips that will have you escaping even the hardest of routes and grips in a matter of time!

- **Be prepared to improvise:** While you should have a plan in place in order to get yourself to safety, more often than not, you will have to improvise as the person attempting to catch you makes every out-of-the-box idea to nab you. Know the difference between choosing escape and survival. Escaping will sometimes mean that you will have to succumb yourself to elements that are not so pleasing. Just remember to balance out the odds and make an educated choice. And once you make a choice, stick with it! Don't become controlled by circumstances when you can avoid them. As you have learned previously, the last thing you should be doing is letting your emotions derail any possible escape route that is open for you.

- **Know yourself:** If you want to have the ability to make hard and fast decisions, you must know yourself and your body. What can you endure? What can you mentally and physically do to escape? You also must know the environment in which you are trapped in. This will help you to weigh the dangers and limitations that you will have to hurdle through.

- **Take opportunities when they are presented:** If you are ever so lucky to have an open door to escape from, even if there are dangers, do your best! Or at least weigh the odds of acting on it or not. Also, when there are opportunities to gather food and hydrate yourself, do not push those times aside, since you never know when another chance to eat and drink will come to you.

- **Blend it:** As a spy, you should know the importance of being able to blend in with the environments, and within the crowds of people you may be in. Use things such as foliage and outdoor resources to hide. If you are being followed in a natural environment, use mud and vegetation to camouflage yourself. In order to successfully blend in, you also need to trust yourself and your instincts. Be aware of the animal life, behavior of the elements and other factors when blending in.

- **Avoid unwanted attention:** There are three main things that will immediately draw attention to you when you least would like it:

- Shiny objects

- Noise

- Any movement that will draw the eye towards your whereabouts

Successful Evasion

Here are some tips crucial to your success in evading your enemy.

Know the surroundings

Be proactive by gathering intel on the location you are visiting, as well as dangerous and safe areas nearby. This will help you to think of a plan if you are captured, have managed to escape but have no idea your next move. The more you know, the better off you will be. The enemy already has a home-field advantage, so why provide them with a weak link to take advantage of?

Utilize social engineering to your advantage

Earlier in this book, you learned quite a bit about the ins and outs of successful social engineering. Well, if you need to evade your enemy, now is a great time to put those skills to use! You can use these skills to manipulate people into providing you with things if you are trapped in a desperate situation.

Prevent stress when possible

As you have previously learned, one of the biggest reasons that people die in dangerous scenarios is the simple fact that they let stress fuel their emotions and thoughts. This is why, especially as a spy, it is so imperative that you practice those skills on a regular basis, so that you mold your mind into typically thinking, even in high-stress situations. The key is to keep your heart rate down. The higher it goes, the less motor skills and cognitive abilities you have to work with.

Create hidden supplies

Creating and hiding hidden tools and supplies can be the difference between life and death. This includes anything from medical kits, water, weapons, money, food, etc. Some of the best ways to hide these things are within buckets, PVC pipes with capped ends, cammo cans, Ziploc bags, you get the idea. It is a good idea to make more than one stashing place so that if your hiding spot is discovered, you are not out of luck.

Utilize disguises

We have previously discussed about using the environment to go unseen. The same goes for more urban-like areas. In big cities, there are homeless folks and hookers. Even though they are highly noticeable, people tend to not look at them to prevent nasty responses. There are also people such as construction workers, mailmen, and serve people that blend in very well with the surroundings.

69

As a spy, fake ID's are a goldmine of opportunities if something does not go according to plan. If you cannot do that, learn how to blend it via the information we have previously discussed, or by finding disguises that will help your enemy overlook you.

Improvise choice of weapons

In the course of evasion, you typically do not get to take a nice and packed backpack full of gear with you. Knowing this, you should be prepared for creative thinking. Look around you, what can be potentially used as a weapon? Grab it and use it when needed. There are many things, especially in urban places, lying around that can be used as a weapon.

Survival Driving Tips

If you are lucky enough to find a car or other type of moving vehicle during your escape and evade plan, this chapter discusses some things to keep in mind as you make your way out of the city or countryside in which you were being held and how to stay away from the wandering eyes of other people working for the enemy.

Defensively Drive

This is a tip you have learned from day one of driving school, but it applies to every aspect of being behind the wheel, even during evasion. Even though you are in a hurry to escape from your captor, you do not need to do so in a NASCAR style. The last thing you need is to get into an accident and be captured again. Besides the fact, if you drive normal, you are less likely to be found and seen by the enemy, who is looking out for a stressed driver.

Keep Your Distance

This tip goes two ways. If you are tailing a criminal and attempting to catch them in the act, don't go driving right behind them. Instead, keep a few cars between you, or at least some distance so that they do not become suspicious.

Also, if you are evading an enemy, it is best to keep your distance from other cars and drive as normally as possible, to prevent accidents or attracting unwanted attention to yourself.

Keep Your Composure

If you have found a car to get away in, make sure that in the height of this excitement to keep your composure. Even the most trained spies can lose their cool when their minds are running 100 miles per hour. Learn how to multitask, driving normally while still concocting a plan to evade the enemy.

Learn Value of Timing

If you manage to find a car to get away in, but the enemy is close, it might be best to hide within the car but don't start it up and drive off erratically. This is just the type of movement your enemy is looking for. Hunker down for awhile and wait it out. That way, you can create a plan for what to do next, while still having an escape route.

Also, learn when it is time to ditch the car and get yourself to a safer area or take public transportation. If you stay in the same vehicle for too long, your enemy could easily track you and hunt you down when you least expect them to.

Conclusion

Congratulations! You have made it to the end of *How to Think like a Spy*!

Now that you have read the valuable information tucked within the chapters of this book, I hope that you have a whole new sense of confidence that you really do have what it takes to become an undercover agent!

From gaining the unique perspective of an operative to learning the physical skills that you will likely need to evade enemies and peering eyes, you have acquired exclusive knowledge that is not just a quick Google search away. While you are free to share the intelligence packed in this book, why would you? If you keep all this knowledge to yourself, you can easily one-up a variety of folks in your life.

I hope that this book was able to provide you the tools you desired when you stumbled across this novel. Your dream to become an agent is no longer a far reach, but rather a desire much closer that you have the ability to realistically achieve.

So, what do you do next? As the reader of this

book, you will never know how beneficial this material is unless you put it to the test in everyday life! You have nothing to lose and much to gain from putting these tips and tricks to the test. If you are worried about failure, don't be. While you may have to try out some methods a few times, you will eventually get the expertise it takes to use this intelligence to your advantage.

Did you find this book fun to read, useful, and/or valuable in any way? If so, please take a moment from your spy sleuthing to head over to Amazon and leave a review! It's highly appreciated. Good luck, my informant friend!

Printed in Great Britain
by Amazon

84786101R00047